Rookie
biographies®

Booker T. Washington

By Christine Taylor-Butler

Reading Consultant
Cecilia Minden-Cupp, PhD
Former Director of the Language and Literacy Program
Harvard Graduate School of Education
Cambridge, Massachusetts

Children's Press®
A Division of Scholastic Inc.
New York   Toronto   London   Auckland   Syd
Mexico City   New Delhi   Hong Kong
Danbury, Connecticut

Designer: Herman Adler Design
Photo Researcher: Caroline Anderson
The photo on the cover shows Booker T. Washington.

Library of Congress Cataloging-in-Publication Data

Taylor-Butler, Christine.
  Booker T. Washington / by Christine Taylor-Butler.
    p. cm. — (Rookie biographies)
  Includes index.
  ISBN-10: 0-516-29842-9 (lib. bdg.)   0-516-27302-7 (pbk.)
  ISBN-13: 978-0-516-29842-9 (lib. bdg.)   978-0-516-27302-0 (pbk.)
  1. Washington, Booker T., 1856–1915—Juvenile literature. 2. African Americans—
Biography—Juvenile literature. 3. Educators—United States—Biography—Juvenile
literature. I. Title. II. Rookie biography.
  E185.97.W4T395 2006
  370'.92—dc22   2005030251

Do you believe you can do anything if you work hard enough? Booker T. Washington believed that he could.

Booker T. Washington sits in his office in 1902.

African American workers planting sweet potatoes on a plantation in South Carolina in 1862

Washington believed that people should work hard to make their lives better. He helped former African American slaves get an education and find jobs.

Washington was born on a Virginia tobacco farm in 1856. His mother was a slave on the farm. Washington's father was a white farmer who lived nearby.

Booker T. Washington was born in this cabin in Virginia.

A slave family working in a cotton field in the 1860s

Washington was forced to work as a slave on the same farm as his mother. Sometimes he carried schoolbooks for the farmer's daughter.

Washington wished he could go to school, but slaves were not allowed to get an education.

President Abraham Lincoln ordered that all slaves be freed in 1865. This was called the Emancipation Proclamation (i-MAN-si-pay-shuhn pruh-kluh-MAY-shuhn).

Then Washington and his family moved to Malden, West Virginia. Washington was finally able to go to school.

Abraham Lincoln was the sixteenth president of the United States.

Freed slaves attending school in 1870

Washington took a job in the salt mines to help his family. He was only nine years old. Washington began work at 4 A.M. so that he could finish his job in the mines before he went to school.

Washington began attending the Hampton Institute in 1872. This was a new school for African Americans in Hampton, Virginia.

Washington graduated from the Hampton Institute in 1875 and became a teacher in Malden.

Former slaves learned printing at the Hampton Institute. They then used this skill to print newspapers and books.

The Tuskegee Institute started with only a few buildings.

Washington moved to Tuskegee, Alabama, in 1881.

The state of Alabama gave him $2,000 to start a college for African American students. Washington opened the Tuskegee Institute in 1881.

The Tuskegee Institute began with only one teacher and thirty students.

Washington worked hard to improve the school and to attract more students and teachers. By 1900, the school had more than 1,900 students.

Students working in the lab at the Tuskegee Institute in 1884

Students at the Tuskegee Institute learned the important skill of growing crops.

Students at the Tuskegee Institute learned about farming and business. They produced their own food. They built all the school buildings.

Washington believed African Americans should have the same rights as everyone else. He gave a famous speech in Atlanta in 1895. He said people of different races could work together even if they stayed separate in their private lives.

Washington became very popular with whites and many African Americans.

Washington giving a speech in Pine Bluff, Arkansas

23

W. E. B. DuBois

Other African American leaders
such as W. E. B. DuBois
disagreed with Washington.
DuBois believed African
Americans should be equal in
all ways to whites. He thought
Washington hurt blacks by
saying they could be separate
but equal.

Washington agreed, but he knew it would take awhile for many whites to feel the same way.

In the meantime, Washington secretly donated money to efforts that helped African Americans gain equal rights. He also helped change laws that were unfair to them.

Washington (second from right) hoped businessmen and political leaders such as (from left to right) R. C. Ogden, William Taft, and Andrew Carnegie would help him improve life for African Americans.

28

Booker T. Washington received
a special degree from Harvard
University in 1896. He wrote
twelve books about his
life experiences.

Washington died on
November 14, 1915, at the
age of fifty-nine.

People of all races continue
to respect him today.

Words You Know

Abraham Lincoln

Booker T. Washington

Hampton Institute

slaves

Tuskegee Institute

W. E. B. DuBois

31

Index

African Americans, 4, 5, 8, 14, 17, 22, 25, 26
birth, 6, 7
business, 21
childhood, 9, 13
death, 29
DuBois, W. E. B., 24, 25
education, 5, 9, 10, 12, 13–14, 17–18
Emancipation Proclamation, 10
equality, 25–26
farming, 6, 8, 9, 20, 21
father, 6
Hampton Institute, 14, 15
Hampton, Virginia, 14

Harvard University, 29
jobs, 5, 13
laws, 26
Lincoln, Abraham, 10, 11
Malden, West Virginia, 10, 14
mother, 6
plantations, 4
rights, 22
salt mining, 13
slavery, 5, 6, 9–10
teachers, 14, 18
tobacco farming, 6, 9
Tuskegee, Alabama, 17
Tuskegee Institute, 16, 17–18, 19, 21

About the Author

Christine Taylor-Butler is the author of more than twenty-four books for children. A graduate of the Massachusetts Institute of Technology, she now lives in Kansas City, Missouri, where she teaches her own children about the importance of history and the value of education.

Photo Credits

Photographs © 2007: Corbis Images: 8, 16, 30 bottom, 31 bottom left (Bettmann), 11, 30 top left; Getty Images/Hulton Archive: 4 (H.P. Moore), 12, 19 (MPI); Library of Congress: 3, 20, 30 top right (Frances Benjamin Johnston), cover, 23, 27; North Wind Picture Archives: 7 (Nancy Carter), 15, 31 top; The Art Archive/Picture Desk/Culver Pictures: 24, 28, 31 bottom right.